A nap

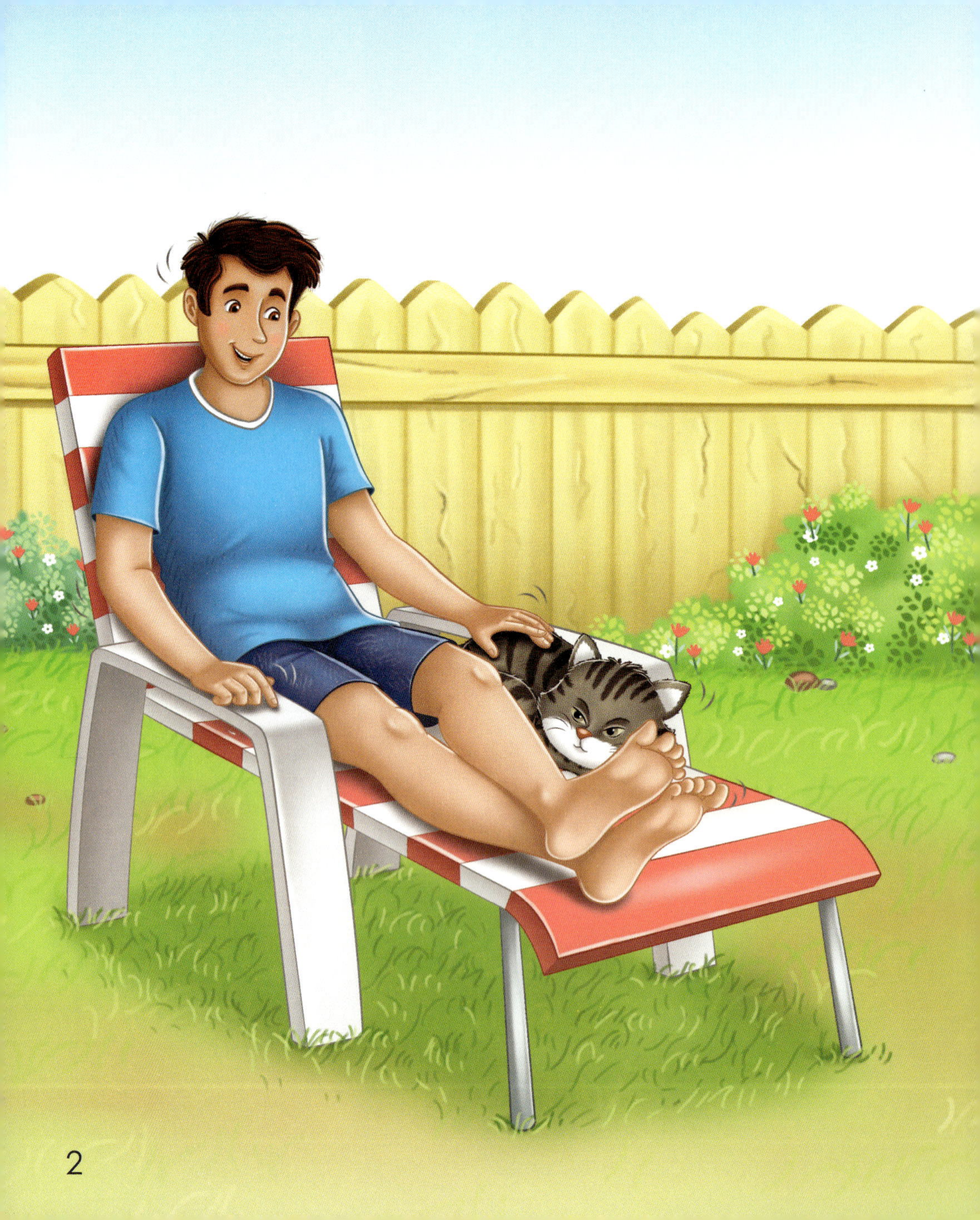

Dad pats Sid.

4

Sid and Dad nap.

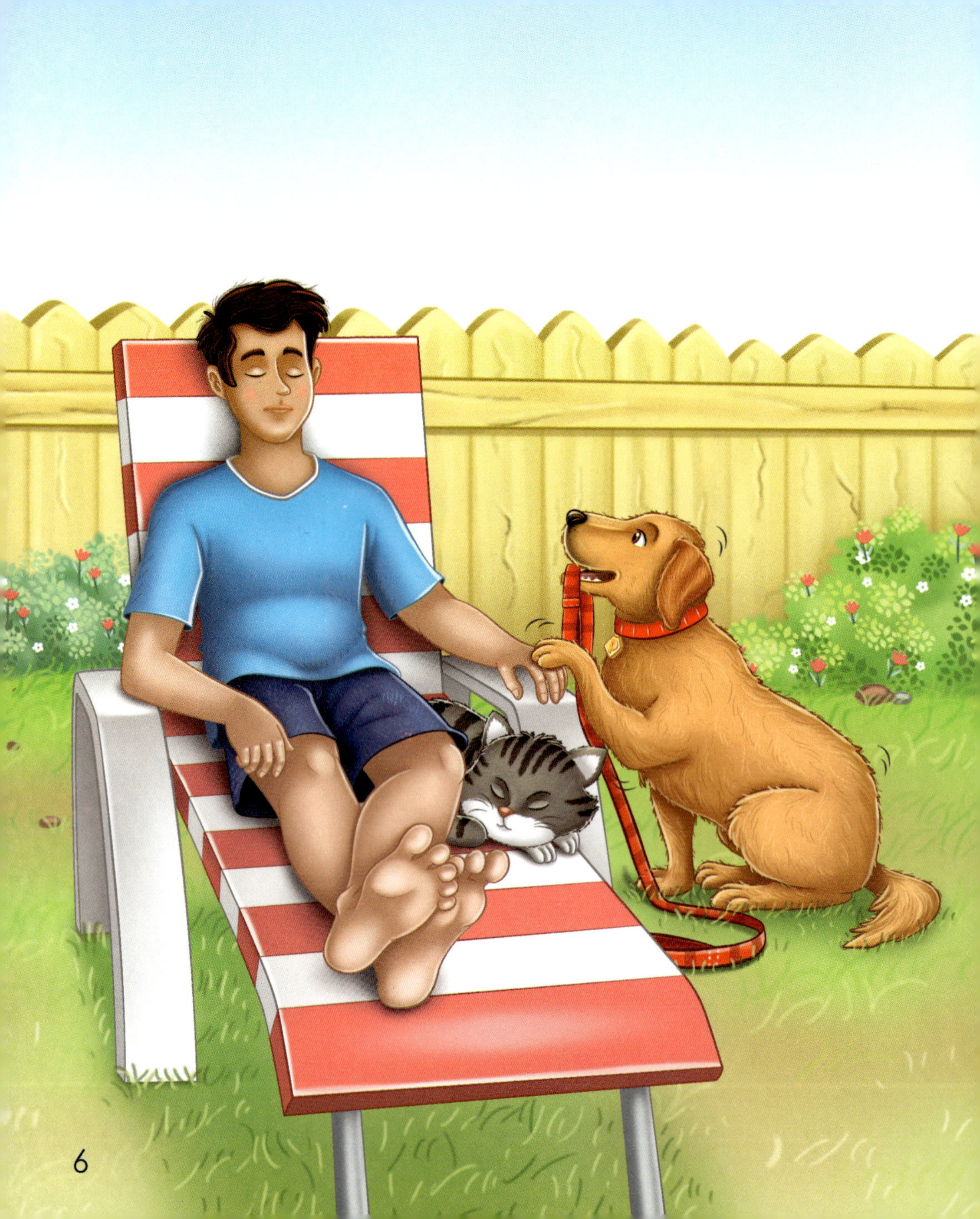

Pam taps Dad.

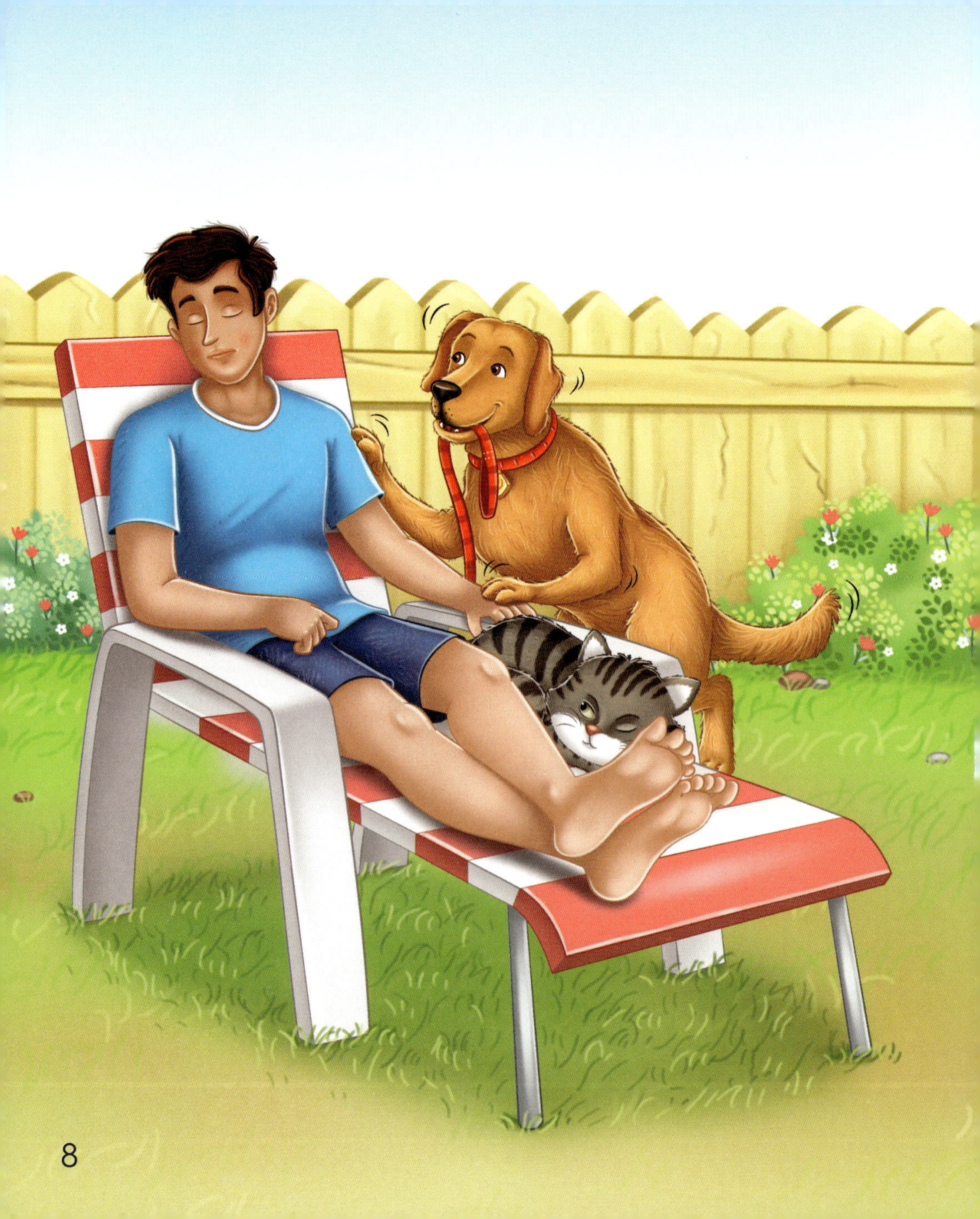

Tap, tap, tap.

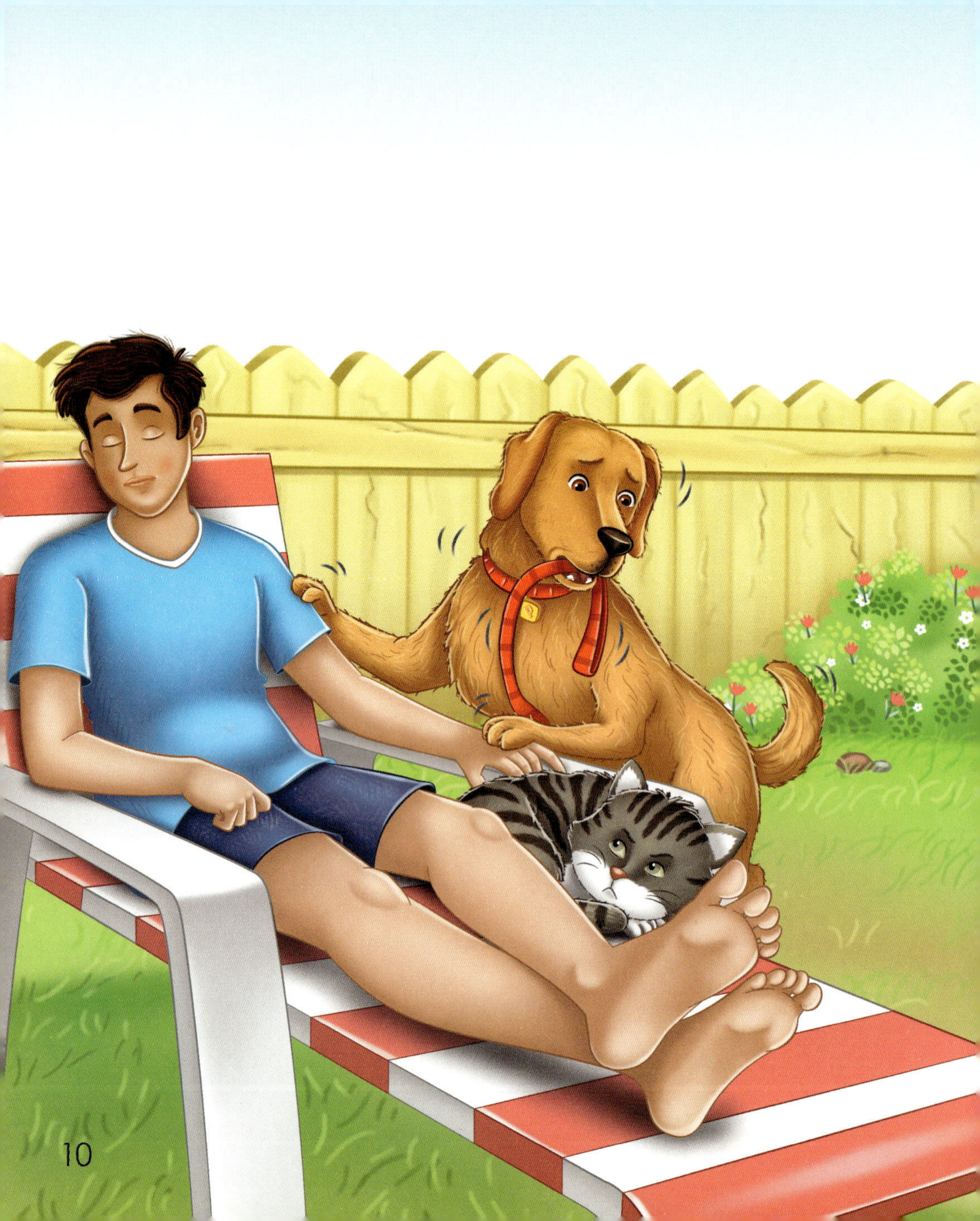

Dad naps.

12

Sid taps Pam.

14

Tap, tap, tap.

A nap

Level 1, Set 2: Story 5

Before reading

Say the sounds: s a t p i n m d
Ensure the children use pure sounds for the consonants without the added "uh" sounds, e.g. "mmmm" not "muh".

Practise blending the sounds: nap Dad pats Sid Pam taps naps tap
High-frequency words: a **Tricky words:** and
Vocabulary check: tap – to hit lightly

Story discussion: Who is having a nap in the cover picture? Where are they?

Teaching points: Introduce A/a as a high-frequency word. Explain that when "a" is used as a word, it can sometimes have a different sound to the /a/ in words like "tap" and "nap".
Check that children can recognise commas and know how to pause slightly at a comma when reading.

After reading

Comprehension:
- Are Dad and Sid enjoying their nap?
- How do they feel about being woken up?
- What do Pam and Sid do at the end of the story?
- Is Dad cross, or does he think it's funny?

Fluency: Speed-read the words from the inside front cover.